MIAMI HEAT

CHARLIE BEATTIE

WWW.APEXEDITIONS.COM

Apex is distributed by North Star Editions:
sales@northstareditions.com | 888-417-0195

Produced for Apex by Red Line Editorial.

Photographs ©: Matt Slocum/AP Images, cover, 1; Gregory Shamus/Getty Images Sport/Getty Images, 4–5, 6–7; Mike Powell/Getty Images Sport/Getty Images, 8–9; Mark Elias/AP Images, 10–11; Andy Lyons/Allsport/Getty Images Sport/Getty Images, 12–13; Eliot J. Schechter/Getty Images Sport/Getty Images, 14–15, 38–39; Otto Greule Jr./Getty Images Sport/Getty Images, 17; Tim De Frisco/Allsport/Getty Images Sport/Getty Images, 18–19; Focus On Sport/Getty Images Sport/Getty Images, 20–21; Bernie Nunez/Getty Images Sport/Getty Images, 22–23; Harry How/Getty Images Sport/Getty Images, 24–25; Donna McWilliam/AP Images, 26–27, 58–59; Mike Ehrmann/Getty Images Sport/Getty Images, 28–29, 32–33; Lynne Sladky/AP Images, 30–31, 52–53; Stacy Revere/Getty Images Sport/Getty Images, 34–35; Morry Gash/AP Images, 37, 57; Marc Serota/Getty Images Sport/Getty Images, 40–41; Doug Benc/Getty Images Sport/Getty Images, 42–43; Jason Miller/Getty Images Sport/Getty Images, 44–45; Drew Hallowell/Getty Images Sport/Getty Images, 47; Michael Reaves/Getty Images Sport/Getty Images, 48–49; Shutterstock Images, 50–51; Marc Pesetsky/AP Images, 54–55

Library of Congress Control Number: 2025939406

ISBN
979-8-89250-908-4 (hardcover)
979-8-89250-939-8 (paperback)
979-8-89824-015-8 (ebook pdf)
979-8-89250-970-1 (hosted ebook)

Printed in the United States of America
Mankato, MN
012026

NOTE TO PARENTS AND EDUCATORS

Apex books are designed to build literacy skills in striving readers. Exciting, high-interest content attracts and holds readers' attention. The text is carefully leveled to allow students to achieve success quickly.

TABLE OF CONTENTS

CHAPTER 1

LET'S GO HEAT!

Time was running out on the Miami Heat. They were facing the Detroit Pistons in a March 2024 game. The score was tied 101–101. Miami guard Terry Rozier tried driving to the hoop. But two defenders stopped him. Rozier had to think fast.

Terry Rozier recorded 17 points and 9 assists against the Detroit Pistons on March 17, 2024.

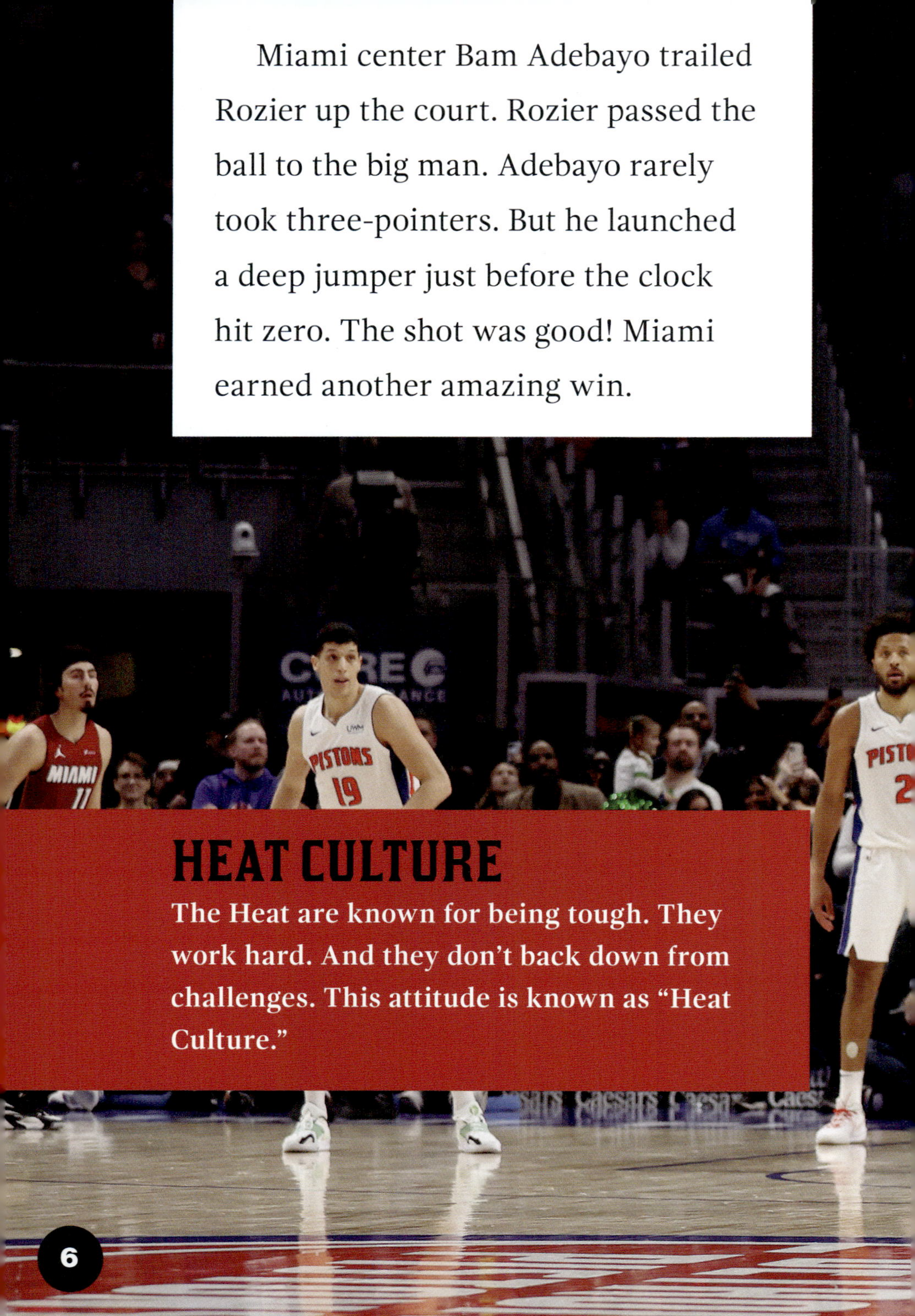

Miami center Bam Adebayo trailed Rozier up the court. Rozier passed the ball to the big man. Adebayo rarely took three-pointers. But he launched a deep jumper just before the clock hit zero. The shot was good! Miami earned another amazing win.

HEAT CULTURE

The Heat are known for being tough. They work hard. And they don't back down from challenges. This attitude is known as "Heat Culture."

Bam Adebayo hits a buzzer-beater from downtown, lifting the Heat to a thrilling victory.

CHAPTER 2

EARLY HISTORY

In the late 1980s, the National Basketball Association (NBA) was ready to grow. The league was popular with fans. The Miami Heat were one of four expansion teams. They played their first season in 1988–89.

Miami power forward Grant Long competes in a 1988 game against the Los Angeles Lakers.

Heat guard Steve Smith attempts a layup during a 1992 playoff game against the Chicago Bulls.

The Heat struggled at first. They had losing records in their first four seasons. But in their fourth season, they finished 38–44. That was good enough to make the playoffs. However, Miami lost in the first round.

FLORIDIANS

The Heat were Miami's second pro basketball team. The Miami Floridians played in the American Basketball Association (ABA). They lasted from 1968 to 1972.

The Heat made some big trades to improve the team. They brought in Alonzo Mourning and Tim Hardaway. Soon, Miami became known for its tough defense. In 1997, the Heat won a playoff series for the first time. They made it all the way to the conference finals.

KNICKS RIVALRY

The Heat had a huge rivalry with the New York Knicks in the 1990s. The teams met in the playoffs every year from 1997 to 2000. The games were tough and physical. Miami won the first year. The Knicks won the next three.

Tim Hardaway drives past a defender during a 1997 playoff game against the New York Knicks.

The Heat struggled in the early 2000s. The team went 25–57 in 2002–03. That summer, Miami drafted guard Dwyane Wade. In his first season, Wade led Miami back to the playoffs. The Heat won their first series. Miami beat the New Orleans Hornets in seven games.

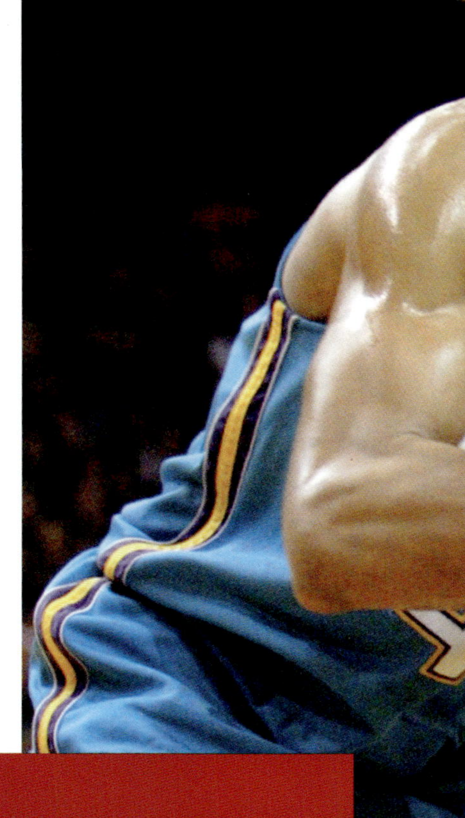

CLUTCH SHOT

Miami's first playoff game in 2004 went down to the wire. The Heat were tied 79–79 with the New Orleans Hornets. Rookie Dwyane Wade drained the game-winning shot with one second left. It was the first of many big shots in his career.

Lamar Odom averaged 16.3 points per game in the 2004 series against the Hornets.

ALONZO MOURNING

Alonzo Mourning began his career with the Charlotte Hornets. In 1995, he joined the Heat. The center was a great scorer. But he was even better on defense. Mourning led the league in blocked shots in 1998–99 and 1999–2000. He won the Defensive Player of the Year Award both seasons.

Mourning left the NBA in 2002. He needed treatment for a rare disease. But he returned to the league a year later. And in 2005, he came back to the Heat. Mourning helped Miami win the NBA title in 2006.

MOURNING MADE THE ALL-STAR TEAM SEVEN TIMES.

HEAT

CHAPTER 3

LEGENDS

In 1988, Miami used its first-ever draft pick on Rony Seikaly. The center spent six seasons with the Heat. Seikaly had great moves on offense. He also pulled down lots of rebounds.

Rony Seikaly averaged 15.4 points and 10.4 rebounds per game with the Heat.

Miami drafted forward Glen Rice in 1989. Rice was a great shooter. He became the first Heat player to average more than 20 points per game in a season. Shooting guard Steve Smith played alongside Rice. Smith made the All-Rookie Team in 1991–92.

TAKING CHARGE

Grant Long was an original member of the Heat. The forward was a strong rebounder. He was also great at drawing charging calls on opponents. Teammates called him the "Take Charge Man."

Glen Rice piled up 9,248 points in six seasons with the Heat.

Miami traded Rice to the Charlotte Hornets in late 1995. In return, the Heat got Alonzo Mourning. A few months later, the Heat traded for point guard Tim Hardaway. They added forward Jamal Mashburn the next year. These three stars led Miami to the playoffs for four seasons in a row.

ENERGY MAN

Forward Keith Askins joined the Heat in 1990. He played with the team for nine seasons. Askins gave the Heat energy on defense. He also served as the team's captain for four years.

Jamal Mashburn takes it to the rack during a 1997 game against the New Jersey Nets.

Eddie Jones joined the Heat in the early 2000s. He was a solid scorer for six seasons with Miami. Jones teamed with superstar rookie Dwyane Wade in 2003–04. Wade and Jones lifted the Heat back to the playoffs. Forward Lamar Odom helped, too. He led the Heat in rebounds.

MASTER OF MIAMI

The Heat hired Pat Riley in 1995. Riley was Miami's head coach. He was also the team's president. He made trades and signed players. Riley stopped coaching in 2008. But he remained the Heat's president.

Eddie Jones shoots over a Los Angeles Clippers defender in 2004.

CHAPTER 4

RECENT HISTORY

Center Shaquille O'Neal joined the Heat in 2004. He helped Miami become a top team. The Heat reached the 2006 NBA Finals. They beat the Dallas Mavericks in six games. For the first time, the Heat were champions!

The Heat celebrate after winning their first NBA title.

In 2010, the Heat made some big moves. Superstar forward LeBron James joined the team. So did All-Star center Chris Bosh. The Heat were one of the NBA's most exciting teams. They reached the 2011 Finals. But Miami lost to the Mavericks.

THE DECISION

In 2010, LeBron James was the NBA's biggest star. He was a free agent that year. Every team wanted him. James announced his choice during a one-hour TV show. It was called *The Decision*. James picked the Heat.

LeBron James throws down a dunk in Game 1 of the 2011 Finals.

The crowd goes wild after watching Ray Allen (34) hit a game-tying three-pointer.

The Heat made it back to the Finals in 2012. This time, they came out on top. Miami beat the Oklahoma City Thunder in five games. In 2013, the Heat returned to the Finals. The San Antonio Spurs led the series three games to two. In Game 6, the Spurs held a 95–92 lead. But Miami guard Ray Allen hit a clutch three-pointer. The Heat won in overtime. Then they won Game 7.

Miami reached the Finals again in 2014. This time, the Spurs came out on top. James left the Heat after that. By 2017, Bosh and Wade were also gone. Even so, the Heat made a surprising run to the 2020 Finals. However, Miami fell to the Los Angeles Lakers.

IN THE BUBBLE

COVID-19 interrupted the 2019–20 season. No games were played between March 12 and July 30. Every playoff game took place at a sports complex in Florida. Players were not allowed to leave. That way, they would not get sick. It was known as the "NBA Bubble."

Goran Dragić averaged 20.5 points per game in the 2020 conference finals.

In the 2020s, the Heat became a tough defensive team again. Miami returned to the Finals in 2023. But they lost to the Denver Nuggets. Jimmy Butler led the Heat that season. However, he left the team in 2025. Miami started looking for new stars.

PLAYOFF SHOCKER

Miami finished the 2022–23 season with a 44–38 record. They made the playoffs as a No. 8 seed. In the first round, the Heat upset the top-seeded Milwaukee Bucks. It was just the sixth time a No. 8 had beaten a No. 1.

Jimmy Butler dribbles past Bucks superstar Giannis Antetokounmpo during a 2023 playoff game.

DWYANE WADE

Dwyane Wade was one of the top prizes in the 2003 draft. The Heat took him with the fifth pick. Wade had great speed and dribbling skills. He easily beat defenders to the basket. He made the All-Star Game 13 times in 15 seasons with Miami.

Wade led the Heat to the 2006 title. He was named Most Valuable Player (MVP) of the Finals. He also starred for Miami's 2012 and 2013 championship teams. Wade ended his career as the team's leader in points, assists, and steals.

DWYANE WADE SCORED 21,556 POINTS IN HIS 15 SEASONS WITH MIAMI.

MIAMI
3

CHAPTER 5

MODERN STARS

In the 2004–05 season, Miami needed help for Dwyane Wade. So, the team traded for superstar center Shaquille O'Neal. The powerful big man was tough to stop in the paint. In the 2006 Finals, O'Neal helped the Heat win their first title.

Shaquille O'Neal made the All-Star Game in three of his four seasons with the Heat.

LeBron James (6), Chris Bosh (1), and Dwyane Wade (3) led Miami to the Finals four years in a row.

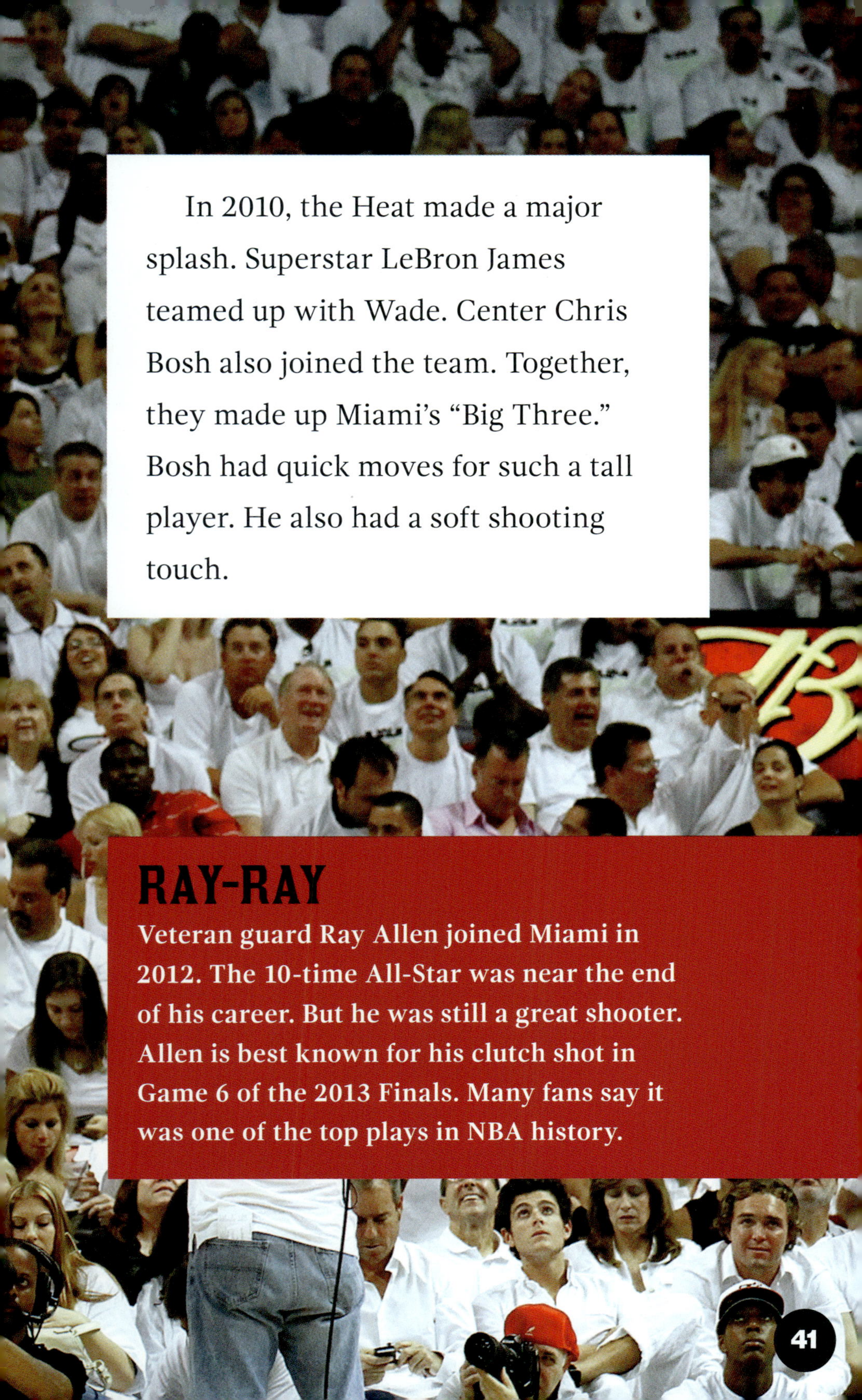

In 2010, the Heat made a major splash. Superstar LeBron James teamed up with Wade. Center Chris Bosh also joined the team. Together, they made up Miami's "Big Three." Bosh had quick moves for such a tall player. He also had a soft shooting touch.

RAY-RAY

Veteran guard Ray Allen joined Miami in 2012. The 10-time All-Star was near the end of his career. But he was still a great shooter. Allen is best known for his clutch shot in Game 6 of the 2013 Finals. Many fans say it was one of the top plays in NBA history.

Hard-working forward Udonis Haslem joined the Heat in 2003. He spent 20 seasons with the team. Haslem ended his career in 2023. He was the Heat's all-time leading rebounder.

COACH SPO

Pat Riley hired Erik Spoelstra as Miami's head coach in 2008. Spoelstra had never been a head coach before. But he led the Heat to NBA titles in 2012 and 2013. In 2025, he finished his 17th season as Miami's coach.

The Heat retired Udonis Haslem's No. 40 jersey in 2024.

Tyler Herro competes in a 2025 playoff game against the Cleveland Cavaliers.

Jimmy Butler carried the Heat to the NBA Finals in 2020 and 2023. The forward was a great scorer. Butler had 13 triple-doubles with the Heat. That was a team record.

Center Bam Adebayo was one of the NBA's top defenders. Guard Tyler Herro was a great outside shooter. The pair led Miami back to the playoffs in 2025.

LeBRON JAMES

LeBron James was already a superstar before he joined the Heat. But he hadn't won an NBA title yet. James soon fixed that. He spent only four seasons with Miami. But he led the team to the Finals each year. Miami won twice.

James had many memorable games with the Heat. One was Game 5 of the 2012 Finals. James recorded 26 points, 11 rebounds, and 13 assists. Miami beat Oklahoma City 121–106 to clinch the title. Game 7 of the 2013 Finals was another big one. James scored 37 points. The Heat won the title again.

LeBRON JAMES WAS NAMED FINALS MVP IN BOTH 2012 AND 2013.

HEAT
SPALDING

CHAPTER 6

TEAM TRIVIA

Miami's mascot is named Burnie. The orange character looks like a fireball. His nose is a green basketball. Burnie has been the Heat's mascot since 1988.

Burnie fires up Heat fans during Miami's home games.

The Heat's arena can hold more than 19,000 fans.

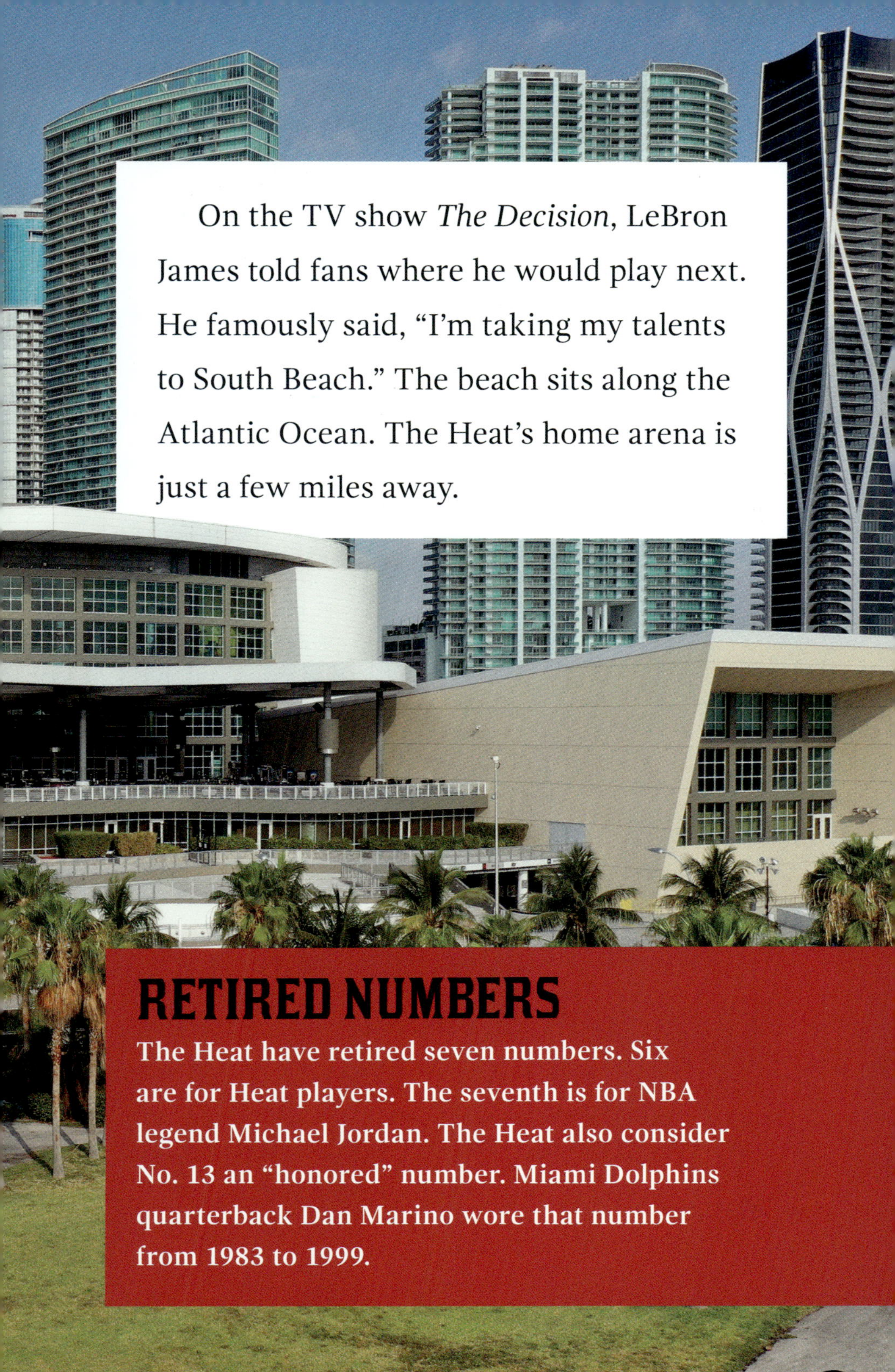

On the TV show *The Decision*, LeBron James told fans where he would play next. He famously said, "I'm taking my talents to South Beach." The beach sits along the Atlantic Ocean. The Heat's home arena is just a few miles away.

RETIRED NUMBERS

The Heat have retired seven numbers. Six are for Heat players. The seventh is for NBA legend Michael Jordan. The Heat also consider No. 13 an "honored" number. Miami Dolphins quarterback Dan Marino wore that number from 1983 to 1999.

Bam Adebayo sports a blue and pink uniform during a 2020 game.

Miami Vice was a popular TV show in the 1980s. The Heat were almost named the Vice. For some games, the Heat wear blue and pink uniforms. These colors honor the show. Many characters wore colorful clothes.

FAMOUS FANS

Many famous people live in Miami. Musicians DJ Khaled and Pitbull often go to Heat games. So does tennis legend Serena Williams. Dwayne "The Rock" Johnson is another Heat superfan.

The Miami Heat and the Orlando Magic both joined the NBA in the late 1980s.

The Heat are one of two NBA teams in Florida. They have a rivalry with the Orlando Magic. The Heat developed other rivalries over the years, too. In the 1990s, they often battled the New York Knicks in the playoffs. The Heat have played the Boston Celtics several times in the conference finals. Miami won in 2012, 2020, and 2023. Boston won in 2022.

TEAM RECORDS

All-Time Points: 21,556
Dwyane Wade (2003–16, 2018–19)

All-Time Assists: 5,310
Dwyane Wade (2003–16, 2018–19)

All-Time Rebounds: 5,791
Udonis Haslem (2003–23)

All-Time Steals: 1,492
Dwyane Wade (2003–16, 2018–19)

All-Time Blocks: 1,625
Alonzo Mourning (1995–2002, 2005–08)

All-Time Three-Pointers: 1,202
Duncan Robinson (2018–)

All-Time Triple-Doubles: 13
Jimmy Butler (2019–25)

All-Time Coaching Wins: 787
Erik Spoelstra (2008–)

NBA MVPs: 2
LeBron James (2011–12, 2012–13)

NBA Championships: 3
2005–06, 2011–12, 2012–13

All statistics are accurate through the 2024–25 season.

MIAMI
3

TIMELINE

1988

On November 5, the Heat play their first-ever game but fall to the Los Angeles Clippers 111–91.

1997

The Heat win a playoff series for the first time and reach the conference finals.

1999

Center Alonzo Mourning wins the first of two straight Defensive Player of the Year Awards.

2006

Miami wins its first title by beating the Dallas Mavericks 95–92 in Game 6 of the NBA Finals.

2010

Superstar LeBron James announces his decision to join the Heat.

The Heat defeat the Oklahoma City Thunder in five games to win another NBA title.

The Heat clinch back-to-back titles with a Game 7 win over the San Antonio Spurs.

Dwyane Wade scores 30 points in his last home game with the Heat, lifting the team to a 122–99 win over the Philadelphia 76ers.

Miami's run to the Finals ends in a Game 6 loss to the Los Angeles Lakers inside the "NBA Bubble."

The No. 8 seed Heat beat the No. 1 seed Milwaukee Bucks in the first round of the playoffs. Miami eventually reaches the Finals.

COMPREHENSION QUESTIONS

Write your answers on a separate piece of paper.

1. Write a paragraph that explains the main ideas of Chapter 4.
2. Who do you think was the greatest player in Heat history? Why?
3. Who was the MVP of the 2006 NBA Finals?
   - **A.** Alonzo Mourning
   - **B.** LeBron James
   - **C.** Dwyane Wade
4. Why did the Heat honor Dan Marino's number?
   - **A.** Marino was a legendary athlete in Miami.
   - **B.** Marino helped bring the Heat to Miami.
   - **C.** Marino was the Heat's all-time leading scorer.

5. What does **upset** mean in this book?

In the first round, the Heat ***upset*** *the top-seeded Milwaukee Bucks. It was just the sixth time a No. 8 had beaten a No. 1.*

- **A.** played a team from a different basketball league
- **B.** beat a team that was supposed to be better
- **C.** lost all four games in a playoff series

6. What does **veteran** mean in this book?

Veteran *guard Ray Allen joined Miami in 2012. The 10-time All-Star was near the end of his career.*

- **A.** a fast player who is known for his flashy play
- **B.** a player who has spent several years in a league
- **C.** a young player who is just starting his career

Answer key on page 64.

GLOSSARY

assists
Passes that lead directly to baskets.

conference
A group of teams that make up part of a sports league.

culture
The shared attitudes and ideals within an organization.

drafted
Selected a new player coming into the league.

expansion teams
New teams that are added to a league.

mascot
A figure that is the symbol of a sports team.

retired
Honored a player by deciding that his or her jersey number may not be worn by another player.

rivalry
An ongoing competition that brings out strong emotion from fans and players.

rookie
An athlete in his or her first year as a professional player.

seed
A team's ranking heading into a tournament.

triple-doubles
Games in which a player records at least 10 of three different stats.

TO LEARN MORE

BOOKS

Barry, James. *Miami Heat*. Creative Education, 2025.

Coleman, Ted. *Miami Heat All-Time Greats*. Press Box Books, 2023.

Lilley, Matt. *The NBA Finals*. Apex Editions, 2023.

ONLINE RESOURCES

Visit **www.apexeditions.com** to find links and resources related to this title.

ABOUT THE AUTHOR

Charlie Beattie is a writer, editor, and former sportscaster. Originally from Saint Paul, Minnesota, he now lives in Charleston, South Carolina, with his wife and son.

INDEX

ANSWER KEY:

1. Answers will vary; 2. Answers will vary; 3. C; 4. A; 5. B; 6. B